Carrot Cake

by Sarah Holliday
illustrated by Fred Davy

METCALF ELEMENTA

D0813715

Harcourt

Orlando   Boston   Dallas   Chicago   San Diego

www.harcourtschool.com

Pass the milk.

Pass the butter.

Pass the eggs.

4

Pass the honey.

Pass the carrots.

Pass the fork.

Pass the carrot cake.